U.S. INTERNATIONAL TRADE COMMISSION

Domestic Regulations and U.S. Exports

1. Introduction

Regulations can be costly. If a sector is open to international trade and regulatory compliance costs are borne by producers in one country but not by their foreign competitors, this asymmetry can have a significant effect on international trade flows. The magnitude of the effect depends in part on the specific form of the regulatory compliance costs.

The costs associated with domestic regulations are usually a combination of fixed and variable costs of production. Fixed costs are expenses that do not vary with a firm's output level. They can include overhead expenses, monitoring and reporting requirements, and mandated updating of the technology embodied in plant and equipment. Variable costs, on the other hand, represent expenses that vary directly with a firm's output level. They can include fees or penalties that increase with the level of the firm's output, for example.

Modeling the impact of regulatory compliance costs on export competitiveness requires an economic framework that can include fixed costs as well as variable costs of production. Yet most models of the effects of regulatory policy on trade flows are based on economic models with constant returns to scale and perfect competition that are not structured to allow for fixed costs of production. This assumption dictates the prediction of the economic analysis: an increase in regulatory costs reduces an industry's exports. These models are not equipped to address the changes in fixed costs of production that can result from regulatory changes. Models with increasing returns to scale and monopolistic competition are arguably better suited.

The early "new trade" models of Krugman (1980), Helpman (1981), Helpman and Krugman (1985), and others include fixed and variable costs of production. These models have been extended in Melitz (2003), Helpman, Melitz, and Yeaple (2004), Cheney (2008), and the literature that followed to include fixed costs of exporting and heterogeneity in firms' productivity levels. The models with firm heterogeneity are motivated by evidence that fixed costs of exporting are an important determinant of international trade flows and that exporting firms generally have higher productivity than non-exporting firms.[2]

---

[2] Bernard, Jensen, Redding, and Schott (2007), Tybout (2003), Melitz (2003), and Helpman, Melitz, and Rubinstein (2008) provide evidence on these points.

The model in Chaney (2008) provides a highly tractable framework for analyzing the impact of regulatory costs on a country's exports, though Chaney (2008) does not address that specific issue. Section 2 presents an overview of the model in a partial equilibrium setting. It derives the model's predictions for the changes in exports and imports that would result from an increase in a sector's regulatory compliance costs.

The model predicts that a country-specific increase in fixed costs of production imposed on all domestic firms will have little or no effect on the sector's exports, because exporting firms are generally more productive and will probably be able to maintain profitability despite the increase in fixed costs of production. Non-exporters are the most likely firms to lose profitability and exit the market. The model also predicts that any increase in production costs, whether fixed or variable, will increase a sector's imports. The cost increase reduces the number of domestic producers in equilibrium, and this raises the sector's price index in the domestic market and increases the price competitiveness of imports.

If the increase in the sector's compliance costs is global rather than country-specific, then the increase will generally increase every country's exports, because the cost increase in each market reduces the number of local producers and increases the demand for foreign products. The result is an increase in the range of firms that export to every country and an increase in the total value of international trade. In contrast, the model predicts that a country-specific increase in a sector's variable costs of production will reduce the sector's exports, because it reduces the number of firms that export (a change in the extensive margin) and also the value of exports from the firms that continue to export (a change in the intensive margin).

Section 3 embeds the Melitz-Chaney model in a GTAP Computable General Equilibrium (CGE) model to more fully account for the adjustment in factor prices and for each sector's links to the rest of the global economy. I discuss the new equations and variables that I add to the GTAP model and my calibration strategy, which includes econometric estimation of the new model parameters. Section 4 uses this extended GTAP model to simulate the effects of the labor costs of pollution abatement on trade, production, and employment in the electronics, machinery, and transportation equipment sectors in the United States. This application is one illustration of the simulation model, but the model can be used to evaluate the effects of a variety of behind-the-border non-tariff measures that are structured in part as fixed costs of production. Section 5 provides concluding remarks.

2. Melitz-Chaney Model in a Partial Equilibrium Setting

The theoretical framework is based on the model of international trade with monopolistic competition, firm heterogeneity, and fixed costs of production and exporting in Melitz (2003), as it is extended in Chaney (2008). After introducing the assumptions of the Melitz-Chaney model, I derive the changes in international trade flows that would result from an increase in a sector's fixed and variable costs of production.

2.1 Overview of the Melitz-Chaney Model

In the partial equilibrium model, there are several sectors that produce differentiated goods and one sector that produces a homogeneous good. Labor is the only factor of production. Labor in country j earns the wage w_j. There are constant returns to scale and no fixed costs of production in the sector that produces the homogeneous good. In the extensions of the Melitz model in Helpman, Melitz, and Yeaple (2004) and Chaney (2008), the wage in each country is fixed by free trade in the homogeneous good. Under this simplifying assumption, each differentiated goods sector can be modeled in isolation. In this section, I limit the model to two countries. I relax these three simplifying restrictions – labor as the only factor of production, wages that do not adjust to factor requirements in the differentiated goods sectors, and only two countries – in the CGE analysis in Section 3.

In contrast, the cost structure for the differentiated goods includes fixed costs as well as variable costs of production. Within each of the differentiated goods sectors, the firms vary in their productivity parameter φ. $G(\varphi)$ is the cumulative distribution function of the productivity of firms in each sector in each country. Each firm in country j incurs a fixed overhead cost of production, f_{Dj} units of labor, regardless of its level of output. This overhead cost includes, but is not limited to, some types of regulatory compliance costs. The firms in these sectors exhibit increasing returns to scale due to the fixed costs of production. The firms have constant marginal costs of production. Each firm in country j incurs an additional fixed cost, f_{Xj} units of labor, if it exports its product. This reflects the cost of establishing a distribution and servicing network in the foreign country.

In the models in Melitz (2003) and Helpman, Melitz, and Yeaple (2004), the number of potential producers is determined by entry decisions. Potential entrants weigh one-time entry costs against uncertain future profits. Once a firm pays the entry costs, it draws its firm-specific productivity. In contrast, the model in Chaney (2008) treats the number of potential producers as an exogenous parameter, though the numbers of firms that decide to actually produce and sell in the domestic and export markets are endogenously determined, conditional on the set of potential producers. I adopt Chaney's assumption, since it is a better match for the deterministic GTAP CGE model.

Equation (1) represents the domestic demand for the products of a firm in country j with productivity parameter φ. Consumer demand in each country has a constant elasticity of substitution between the varieties of products within each sector, represented by σ.[3]

$$q_{Dj}(\varphi) = \mu\, Y_j\, P_j^{\sigma-1} \left(p_{Dj}(\varphi)\right)^{-\sigma} \tag{1}$$

The variable $p_{Dj}(\varphi)$ is the domestic price of a firm with productivity φ. Y_j is aggregate expenditure in country j, P_j is the sector's price index in country j, and μ is the sector's share of aggregate expenditures.[4] In equilibrium, there is a continuum of varieties produced by a continuum of firms. Each producer takes the sector's price index, the sector's expenditure share, and aggregate expenditure as given when setting its own price. The firm's profit-maximizing price is characterized by the constant mark-up formula in equation (2).

$$p_{Dj}(\varphi) = \left(\frac{\sigma}{\sigma-1}\right)\frac{w_j}{\varphi} \tag{2}$$

Equation (3) represents the firm's profits from domestic sales in country j.

$$\pi_{Dj}(\varphi) = \left[p_{Dj}(\varphi) - \frac{w_j}{\varphi}\right] q_{Dj}(\varphi) - f_{Dj}\, w_j \tag{3}$$

---

[3] To simplify the notation, I do not include a subscript for the sector or the time period in the equations that follow.

[4] The constant expenditure shares of each sector reflect the model's assumption that the elasticity of substitution between the sectors is equal to one.

The firm's decision to supply the domestic market, rather than exit, depends on the profitability of market participation. The firm pays the fixed cost $f_{Dj} w_j$ and sells its product in the domestic market if the firm's productivity is high enough that $\pi_{Dj}(\varphi) > 0$. This is the case if the firm's productivity φ is greater than the cutoff level φ_{Dj} defined in equation (4).

$$\varphi_{Dj} = \left[(f_{Dj}) \, (w_j)^\sigma \, (\mu \, Y_j)^{-1} (P_j)^{1-\sigma} (\sigma)^\sigma (\sigma - 1)^{1-\sigma} \right]^{\frac{1}{\sigma - 1}} \tag{4}$$

Equation (5) represents the demand in country k for the exports of a firm in country j with productivity φ.

$$q_{Xj}(\varphi) = \mu \, Y_k \, P_k^{\sigma - 1} \left(p_{Xj}(\varphi) \right)^{-\sigma} \tag{5}$$

Exports to country k are subject to iceberg trade costs, represented by $\lambda_{jk} > 1$. The trade costs create a wedge between the firm's price in its domestic market and its price in its export market: $p_{Xj}(\varphi) = \lambda_{jk} \, p_{Dj}(\varphi)$. Equation (6) represents the firm's incremental profits from exporting, assuming that the firm has already incurred the fixed cost of production to sell in its domestic market.

$$\pi_{Xj}(\varphi) = \left(\left[p_{Xj}(\varphi) - \lambda_{jk} \frac{w_j}{\varphi} \right] q_{Xj}(\varphi) \right) - f_{Xj} \, w_j \tag{6}$$

Equation (7) defines the cutoff productivity level for exporting from country j, φ_{Xj}.

$$\varphi_{Xj} = \left[(f_{Xj}) \, (w_j)^\sigma (\lambda_{jk})^\sigma \, (\mu \, Y_j)^{-1} (P_k)^{1-\sigma} (\sigma)^\sigma (\sigma - 1)^{1-\sigma} \right]^{\frac{1}{\sigma - 1}} \tag{7}$$

Exporting is profitable for firms with $\varphi > \varphi_{Xj}$.

Equation (8) is the sector's CES price index in country j, given the profit-maximizing prices of each firm.

$$P_j = \left(\frac{\sigma}{\sigma - 1} \right) \left[n_j \int_{\varphi_{Dj}}^{\infty} \left[\frac{w_j}{\varphi} \right]^{1-\sigma} dG(\varphi) + n_k \int_{\varphi_{Xk}}^{\infty} \left[\frac{w_k \, \lambda_{kj}}{\varphi} \right]^{1-\sigma} dG(\varphi) \right]^{\frac{1}{1-\sigma}} \tag{8}$$

The variable n_j is the number of firms that are potential producers in the differentiated goods sector in country j. The number of firms in the sector that decide to produce and sell in the domestic market is equal to $n_j \int_{\varphi_{Dj}}^{\infty} dG(\varphi)$, and the number that decide to also export to country k is equal to $n_j \int_{\varphi_{Xj}}^{\infty} dG(\varphi)$. Equation (7) and the country k counterparts to equations (4) and (8) jointly determine φ_{Dk}, φ_{Xj}, and P_k for each of the differentiated goods sectors, conditional on aggregate expenditure, wages, and the number of potential producers.

Melitz (2003) points to extensive evidence that exporting firms are more productive on average than non-exporting firms in the same sector. In terms of the model, this implies that $\varphi_{Xj} > \varphi_{Dj}$. This will be the case as long as the fixed costs of exporting are large relative to the fixed costs of production, aggregate expenditure and the sector's price index in the export markets are relatively small, and variable trade costs are large.

2.2 Comparative Static Analysis of Fixed Costs of Production and Exports

In this section, I derive the model's predictions for the changes in international trade flows that would result from an increase in a sector's fixed costs of production in country j, f_{Dj}. Equations (1) through (8) imply the following solution for X_j, the value of exports from country j aggregated across all of the firms in the sector:

$$X_j = \mu Y_k \frac{n_j \int_{\varphi_{Xj}}^{\infty} \left[\frac{w_j \lambda_{jk}}{\varphi}\right]^{1-\sigma} dG(\varphi)}{n_k \int_{\varphi_{Dk}}^{\infty} \left[\frac{w_k}{\varphi}\right]^{1-\sigma} dG(\varphi) + n_j \int_{\varphi_{Xj}}^{\infty} \left[\frac{w_j \lambda_{jk}}{\varphi}\right]^{1-\sigma} dG(\varphi)} \tag{9}$$

X_j is determined by the value of φ_{Dk} (the cutoff for domestic shipments in country k) and by the value of φ_{Xj} (the cutoff for exports from country j to country k), but not by the value of φ_{Dj} (the cutoff for domestic shipments in country j). Therefore, a moderate increase in f_{Dj} will have no impact on X_j. The number of firms in country j that export is determined independent of f_{Dj} unless there is an increase in f_{Dj} that is so large that it would eliminate all non-exporting producers in country j. Specifically, it would have to raise the cutoff productivity level φ_{Dj} that prevails with the cost increase above the cutoff φ_{Xj} that prevailed absent the cost increase. Otherwise, the exporting firms in country j would be unaffected, because they are relatively productive and remain profitable despite the increase in fixed costs. Since 82% of firms in the U.S. manufacturing sector are not exporters, this would require an improbably large increase in f_{Dj}.[5]

In contrast, the increase in fixed costs of production increases country j's imports in the sector. The cost increase reduces the number of firms that produce in country j. This raises the sector's price index P_j and increases the price competitiveness of imports.

To this point, I have analyzed the changes in international trade flows that would result from a country-specific increase in a sector's fixed costs of production, such as a unilateral increase in regulatory compliance costs. In some cases, however, the increase in fixed costs of production may apply globally. For example, this could be the case if both countries enter into an international regulatory agreement or jointly address regulatory costs in the context of a regional trade agreement. To model this alternative, I assume that the increase in f_{Dj} is matched by an increase in f_{Dk}. The matching increase in the fixed cost of production in country k reduces the number of local producers and raises the sector's price index P_k. This makes country j's exports more price-competitive in country k, and there is an increase in the range of firms that export from country j to country k. According to the model, the global increase in fixed costs of production increases every country's exports.

2.3 Comparative Static Analysis of an Increase in Variable Costs of Production

Finally, I consider the changes in international trade flows that would result from an increase in a sector's variable costs of production. This is an apt description of some types of regulatory compliance costs. A country-specific increase in the variable costs of production significantly reduces the sector's exports, because it reduces the number of firms that export (the extensive margin of the sector's exports) and the value of exports from the firms that continue to export (the intensive margin of the sector's exports). Chaney (2008) emphasizes that adjustment on the extensive margin amplifies the effect of variable costs on trade.[6]

---

[5] This statistic is from Bernard, Jensen, Redding, and Schott (2007).

[6] Chaney (2008) analyzes the impact of a change in variable costs of trade, rather than variable costs of production, but in the context of equation (9), the two are computationally equivalent.

In order to derive a reduced-form expression for X_j, I assume that each firm's productivity parameter is drawn from a Pareto distribution with shape parameter γ, following Helpman, Melitz, and Yeaple (2004) and Chaney (2008). Therefore, $\varphi^{\sigma-1}$ has a Pareto distribution with shape parameter $-\gamma + (\sigma - 1)$. Equation (10) is the reduced-form expression for X_j.

$$X_j = \mu Y_k \frac{n_j (w_j)^{\frac{\sigma-1-\gamma\sigma}{\sigma-1}} (\lambda_{jk})^{-\gamma} (f_{Xj})^{\frac{-\gamma}{\sigma-1}+1}}{n_k (w_k)^{\frac{\sigma-1-\gamma\sigma}{\sigma-1}} (f_{Dk})^{\frac{-\gamma}{\sigma-1}+1} + n_j (w_j)^{\frac{\sigma-1-\gamma\sigma}{\sigma-1}} (\lambda_{jk})^{-\gamma} (f_{Xj})^{\frac{-\gamma}{\sigma-1}+1}} \tag{10}$$

An increase in variable costs of production that is specific to producers in country j has the same effect on X_j as an increase in λ_{jk}, the variable trade cost in equation (10). It reduces the value of exports from country j to country k. The magnitude of the decline in exports is larger if there less dispersion in the distribution of the firms' productivity levels (a higher value of the parameter γ) and if aggregate expenditure in country k is higher.

3. Melitz-Chaney Sectors within a Computable General Equilibrium Framework

In this section, I embed several Melitz-Chaney differentiated goods sectors in the GTAP model to provide a more complete assessment of the economic consequences of increases in fixed costs of production. I use the extended CGE model to quantify the changes in each sector's trade, production, and employment, taking into account the sector's general equilibrium links to the rest of the global economy.

3.1 Modification of the Standard GTAP Model

To facilitate comparison to standard GTAP predictions, I leave most of the structure of the CGE model unchanged, including its multi-tiered demand system, the vertical links between sectors of the economy, and the five-factor production technologies. The structure of the GTAP model is described in detail in Hertel (1997).[7] I aggregate the GTAP dataset to 51 regions, 13 commodity sectors, and 5 factor endowments.[8] Table 1 lists these aggregations.

---

[7] For additional, updated documentation, see https://www.gtap.agecon.purdue.edu/.

[8] The aggregates of countries in the GTAP model are called *regions*, and so I adopt this terminology in the discussion of the CGE model, even in cases where the region is a single country.

As an illustrative example, I assume that 3 of the 13 aggregated sectors in each region are Melitz-Chaney sectors. The three sectors are electronics, machinery, and transportation equipment.[9] These sectors are good candidates, because they account for a significant share of U.S. trade in manufacturing goods and they are separately reported in the GTAP data. They are more likely to fit the Melitz-Chaney differentiated products model than more commoditized products like chemicals and primary metals. I assume that the rest of the economy is characterized by constant returns to scale and the perfect competition market structure of the standard GTAP model.

The first extension of the GTAP model involves defining price indices for the Melitz-Chaney sectors in each region. I replace the sector-level prices in the GTAP model with CES indices of the prices of the individual firms within the sectors. The price indices in the Melitz-Chaney sectors reflect both marginal costs (as in the GTAP model) and the number of firms (the extensive margin from the Melitz-Chaney model). The following equation represents the percentage changes in these price indices in the extended model:

$$\frac{d\left(p_{jm}\right)}{p_{jm}} = \frac{d\left(ps_j\right)}{ps_j} + \left[\left(\frac{\gamma}{\sigma-1}\right) - 1\right]\frac{d\left(\varphi_{jm}\right)}{\varphi_{jm}} \tag{11}$$

The variable p_{jm} is the price index for the region m sales of region j producers, and φ_{jm} is the cutoff productivity level in region j for sales in region m. They are both endogenous variables in the extended model. ps_j is the sector's marginal cost of production in region j, as this variable is defined in the GTAP model.[10] Equation (11) applies in the three Melitz-Chaney sectors; for the other sectors, $p_{jm} = ps_j$ for all m.

---

[9] The machinery sector is the GTAP sector named Machinery and Equipment NEC.

[10] There are five primary factors of production in the GTAP model, but labor is the only factor of production in the models in Melitz (2003) and Chaney (2008). However, this difference is not an obstacle to embedding the Melitz-Chaney model into the GTAP framework. I replace the sector's marginal cost of production ps_j for the wage rate in the Melitz-Chaney model.

The sector price indices vary by the region of consumption as well as the region of production, because there are different sets of firms selling into each region. The following equation represents the percentage changes in the cutoff productivity levels in the extended model:[11]

$$\frac{d\left(\varphi_{jm}\right)}{\varphi_{jm}} = \left[\frac{1}{\sigma-1}\right]\left[\frac{d\left(freq_{jm}\right)}{freq_{jm}} - \frac{d\left(q_{jm}\right)}{q_{jm}} + \frac{d\left(fp_{jm}\right)}{fp_{jm}}\right] - \left[\frac{\sigma}{\sigma-1}\right]\left[\frac{d\left(p_{jm}\right)}{p_{jm}}\right] + \frac{d\left(ps_{j}\right)}{ps_{j}} \qquad (12)$$

The variable $freq_{jm}$ represents the factor requirements for the fixed costs of production in region j (if $j = m$) or the fixed costs of exporting (if $j \neq m$). It is an exogenous variable in the extended model. fp_{jm} is an index of factor prices associated with these fixed costs, and q_{jm} is the volume of region m sales of region j producers.

The second extension of the GTAP model involves the distribution of the profits of the Melitz-Chaney sectors. I assume that the profits of firms located in a region are distributed to households located within the same region.[12] The following equation represents the percentage change in the profitability of each market in the extended model:

$$\frac{d\left(prof_{jm}\right)}{prof_{jm}} = \left[\frac{prof_{jm} + fix_{jm}}{prof_{jm}}\right]\left[\frac{d\left(p_{jm}\right)}{p_{jm}} + \frac{d\left(q_{jm}\right)}{q_{jm}}\right] - \left[\frac{fix_{jm}}{prof_{jm}}\right]\left[\frac{d\left(fp_{jk}\right)}{fp_{jk}} + \frac{d\left(freq_{jm}\right)}{freq_{jm}} - \gamma\frac{d\left(\varphi_{jm}\right)}{\varphi_{jm}}\right]$$

$$(13)$$

$prof_{jm}$ is the dollar value of incremental profits of firms in region j from sales in region m, and fix_{jm} is the total dollar value of their incremental fixed costs of serving the market in region m.

The third extension of the GTAP model involves the use of factor endowments in the fixed costs of production and the fixed costs of exporting. The following equation represents the percentage changes in these additional factor demands in the extended model:

$$\frac{d\left(lfc_{jm}\right)}{lfc_{jm}} = \frac{d\left(freq_{jm}\right)}{freq_{jm}} - \gamma\frac{d\left(\varphi_{jm}\right)}{\varphi_{jm}} \qquad (14)$$

The variable lfc_{jm} is the sector's use of factor endowments for the fixed costs of production (if $j = m$) or the fixed cost of exporting (if $j \neq m$). It is an endogenous variable in the extended

---

[11] Equation (12) assumes that the variable trade cost remains unchanged.
[12] In contrast, Chaney (2008) assumes that consumers in each region own shares in a global portfolio and therefore the profits of firms in each country are distributed globally. It would be straightforward to incorporate this alternative assumption into the extended model.

model. I modify the market clearing conditions for the mobile factor endowments by adding the factor demands represented in equation (14).

3.2 Calibration of the Additional Model Parameters

There are two parameters in the extended model that are not in the standard GTAP model, the shape parameter γ for the Pareto distribution of firms' productivity levels and the elasticity of substitution between the products of different firms within the same sector. In this section, I describe how I calibrate these additional parameters.

First, I set the elasticity of substitution between the varieties of different firms within a sector equal to the elasticity of substitution between the sector's imports from different regions (the parameter ESUBM in the GTAP model), since differentiation between the products of individual firms is the source of differentiation by region in Dixit-Stiglitz models of trade.

Second, I use data on U.S. imports by country and sector to estimate the parameter γ for each of the Melitz-Chaney sectors. Equation (15) is an expression for U.S. imports from country k, based on the model in Section 2. The subscript u represents the United States. I add an index t to indicate time periods.

$$X_{kut} = \frac{\mu_t Y_{ut}}{Z_{ut}} \, n_k \, (w_{kt})^{\frac{\sigma-1-\gamma\sigma}{\sigma-1}} \, (\lambda_{kut})^{-\gamma} (f_{kut})^{\frac{-\gamma}{\sigma-1}+1} \tag{15}$$

where

$$Z_{ut} = n_u \, (w_{ut})^{\frac{\sigma-1-\gamma\sigma}{\sigma-1}} (f_{uut})^{\frac{-\gamma}{\sigma-1}+1} + \sum_{k \neq u} n_k \, (w_{kt})^{\frac{\sigma-1-\gamma\sigma}{\sigma-1}} (\lambda_{kut})^{-\gamma} (f_{kut})^{\frac{-\gamma}{\sigma-1}+1} \tag{16}$$

Equation (17) is a log-linearization of equation (15). It serves as the regression specification.

$$ln(X_{kut}) = \alpha_k + \beta \, ln(\lambda_{kut}) + \delta_t + \varepsilon_{kt} \tag{17}$$

Equations (18) through (21) define the coefficients in equation (17).

$$\alpha_k = ln(n_k) \tag{18}$$

$$\beta = -\gamma \tag{19}$$

$$\delta_t = ln(\mu_t) + ln(Y_{ut}) - ln(Z_{ut}) + \left(\frac{-\gamma}{\sigma-1} + 1\right) ln(f_{kut}) \tag{20}$$

12

$$\varepsilon_{kt} = \left(\frac{\sigma-1-\gamma\sigma}{\sigma-1}\right) ln(w_{kt}) + \xi_{kt} \qquad (21)$$

The variable ξ_{kt} in equation (21) represents measurement error in $ln(X_{kut})$. I assume that the f_{kut} parameters, the fixed costs of exporting from country k to the United States, are the same for all k.

Equation (17) applies separately to each of the Melitz-Chaney sectors. To estimate γ for each sector, I construct a panel dataset that includes imports in the three sectors, from the 50 non-U.S. regions in the extended model, on an annual basis from 2000 to 2009. Table 2 reports the sector-specific estimates of γ for two alternative measures of international trade costs. The first panel of estimates uses a measure of trade costs that is based on the difference between the landed duty-paid value of imports and their customs value, and therefore it includes both freight costs and import duties. The second panel uses a measure of trade costs that is based on the difference between the CIF value of imports and their customs value, and therefore it only includes freight costs. The second measure is preferable if import duties are endogenously determined but independent of freight costs. The estimates in the second panel are slightly larger, as I would expect if the endogeneity of import duties biases the estimates of β toward zero. I use the estimates based on the freight-only measure of trade costs in the simulations in Section 4.

The table reports the point estimates and 95% confidence intervals for each sector's γ parameter. The estimated value of γ is largest for the electronics sector. Both of the specifications include industry-year fixed effects and industry-country fixed effects to control for the unobservable factors in equations (18) and (20). F tests of coefficient restrictions strongly reject the hypotheses that either of these sets of fixed effects are equal to zero.

3.3 Additional Data Inputs

The simulations also require measures of the shares of factor endowments devoted to the fixed costs of production and the fixed costs of exporting. I do not have direct measures of these shares, so I approximate them. I assume that the fixed costs require a fixed ratio of highly skilled and less skilled workers, and that the workers devoted to fixed costs account for approximately 38% of the labor employed in the Melitz-Chaney sectors in each region. 38% is the ratio of the sectors' non-production workers to total employment in the 2007 Economic Census. I allocate

13

75% of these non-production workers to the sector's fixed costs of production and 25% to the sector's fixed costs of exporting. These employment shares enter the profit equations and the factor market clearing equations in the extended model.

4. CGE Simulations of the Effect of Labor Costs of Pollution Abatement on Trade

In this section, I use the extended GTAP model to quantify the impact of a sector's labor costs of pollution abatement on the region's exports, imports, output, employment, profits, factor prices, and the number of firms that serve each region.

4.1 Measuring the Labor Costs of Pollution Abatement in the United States

The 2005 Pollution Abatement Cost and Expenditures (PACE) survey collected information on the 2005 pollution abatement operating costs by category for each NAICS three-digit industry in the U.S. manufacturing sector, as well as the industries' capital expenditures on pollution abatement. Table 3 summarizes this information for the three Melitz-Chaney sectors in the extended model. I report the dollar value of these costs and their share of the sector's total annual costs in the category in the 2005 Annual Survey of Manufactures. Pollution abatement costs measure incremental expenditures on treating, capturing, recycling, disposing of, and preventing air, water, and solid waste pollution. The cost estimates are based on a national probability sample of 20,000 plants in the U.S. manufacturing sector. U.S. Census Bureau (2008) indicates that the PACE data set is the most comprehensive source of information on pollution abatement costs in the U.S. manufacturing sector. The costs include responses to federal, state, and local regulations as well as voluntary initiatives.

For all three sectors, labor costs including contract work account for the majority of the operating costs of pollution abatement. Nevertheless, they only account for a small share of the sectors' overall labor costs, and they are modest relative to the pollution abatement costs of the chemicals and primary metals sectors. Of the three Melitz-Chaney differentiated products sectors in the model, the transportation equipment sector has the largest labor costs of pollution abatement.

4.2 Effect of the Labor Costs of Pollution Abatement

Table 4 reports simulations of the effect of the labor costs of pollution abatement in the three sectors, assuming that these labor costs are fixed costs of production and are country-specific. In all three sectors, the labor costs of pollution abatement result in a small decline in the sector's exports from the United States, with the largest change in the electronics sector. This reflects the sector's relatively large value of γ. In all three sectors, there is an increase in the sector's imports into the United States, with the largest changes in the transportation equipment sector. For each of the sectors, the changes in imports are much larger in absolute value than the changes in exports. The additional labor requirements reduce the sector's volume of output but increase sector employment. They reduce the number of firms that sell to the domestic market and the sector's profits. Overall, the magnitude of the effects on output, employment, profits and imports is largest for the transportation equipment sector, reflecting the relatively large labor costs of pollution abatement in that sector.

4.3 Modeling the Additional Labor Costs as Variable Costs of Production

Table 5 reports simulations that model the labor costs of pollution abatement as variable costs of production rather than fixed costs. Under this alternative assumption, the declines in the sectors' exports and output are much larger, especially in the extended model (i.e., the second column of numbers in Table 5). The changes in sector employment are smaller but still positive in the standard GTAP model (the third column) but negative in the extended model (the second column).

4.4 Global Cost Shocks

In the next set of simulations, I revert to modeling the labor costs of pollution abatement as fixed costs of production, but now I compare the effect of global cost shocks (common to all regions in the model) to the effect of region-specific cost shocks.

Table 6 reports the simulation results for the Electronics sector. When the cost shock is global rather than region-specific, the direction of change in exports is reversed. In the context of the model, a global increase in fixed costs of production increases exports from every region. In contrast, the change in imports is similar whether the labor cost shocks are global or region-specific. When the cost shock is global, the negative effects on the sector's output, profits, and number of domestic producers are smaller, but the positive effects on sector employment are magnified. These patterns are repeated in simulations for the other two Melitz-Chaney sectors. Tables 7 and 8 report the comparison between global and region-specific shocks for the machinery sector and the transportation equipment sector, respectively.

4.5 Sensitivity to the Sector's γ Parameter

Table 9 reports the simulated changes in each sector's U.S. exports and imports in response to a region-specific cost shock for alternative values of γ, assuming that the labor costs of pollution abatement are fixed costs of production. I repeat the simulation results for the point estimate of each sector's parameter from Table 2, and then I report the results using the upper bound of the 95% confidence interval of the sector's γ as a sensitivity analysis. These alternative parameter values do not alter the direction of the changes in the sector's exports and imports, but they increase the absolute magnitudes of the changes in exports.

5. Conclusions

The Melitz-Chaney model generates unconventional predictions about the impact of regulation and other fixed costs of production on international trade flows: an increase in overhead costs may have no effect on a sector's exports and may even increase exports. The specific form of the regulatory compliance costs determines both the direction and the magnitude of the changes in a sector's exports and imports.

The stark predictions of the partial equilibrium model are tempered when it is embedded within the CGE model and adjustments in the prices of factors of production and intermediate goods are taken into account. The labor costs of pollution abatement from the 2005 Pollution Abatement Cost and Expenditures survey provide an illustration of how the model can analyze the effects of domestic regulation on international trade flows. The three sectors that I examine are not especially pollution-intensive, and so the predicted trade, output, and employment effects of the

16

sector- and region-specific labor costs are modest. However, the model is more generally applicable. It can be used to evaluate the effects of a variety of behind-the-border non-tariff measures that are structured in part as fixed costs of production.

The model provides some guidance for the design of regulations, since fixed costs of production have different trade and employment implications than costs that vary with the level of a firm's output. For example, if smaller firms in an industry are exempted from the regulatory costs that larger firms face, then the compliance costs become variable costs of production and have a greater negative impact on the sector's exports and employment. For this reason, when drawing policy conclusions in a specific case, it is important to evaluate the structure of compliance costs along this dimension. Of course, it is also important to assess any benefits of a proposed regulation (like clear air and improved worker safety) in addition to the economic costs that are quantified in my model.

References

Anderson, J.E. and E. van Wincoop, 2003. Gravity with Gravitas: A Solution to the Border Puzzle. American Economic Review 93, 170-192.

Bernard, A.B., J. Eaton, J.B. Jensen, and S. Kortum, 2003. Plants and Productivity in International Trade. American Economic Review 93, 1268-1290.

Bernard, A.B., J.B. Jensen, S.J. Redding, and P.K. Schott, 2007. Firms in International Trade. Journal of Economic Perspectives 21, 105-130.

Bernard, A.B., S.J. Redding, and P.K. Schott, 2007. Comparative Advantage and Heterogeneous Firms. Review of Economic Studies 74, 31-66.

Chaney, T., 2008. Distorted Gravity: The Intensive and Extensive Margins of International Trade. American Economic Review 98, 1707-1721.

Helpman, E., 1981. International Trade in the Presence of Product Differentiation, Economies of Scale, and Monopolistic Competition: A Chamberlin-Heckscher-Ohlin Approach. Journal of International Economics 11, 305-340.

Helpman, E. and P. Krugman, 1985. Market Structure and Foreign Trade. MIT Press, Cambridge.

Helpman, E., M.J. Melitz, and S.R. Yeaple, 2004. Export Versus FDI with Heterogeneous Firms. American Economic Review 94, 300-316.

Helpman, E., M.J. Melitz, and Y. Rubinstein, 2008. Estimating Trade Flows: Trading Partners and Trading Volumes. Quarterly Journal of Economics 123, 441-487.

Hertel, T.W., ed., 1997. Global Trade Analysis: Modeling and Applications. Cambridge University Press, New York.

Krugman, P., 1980. Scale Economies, Product Differentiation, and the Pattern of Trade. American Economic Review 70: 950-959.

Melitz, M.J., 2003. The Impact of Trade on Aggregate industry Productivity and Intra-Industry Reallocations. Econometrica 71, 1695-725.

Tybout, J.R., 2003. Plant and Firm-Level Evidence on 'New' Trade Theories, in E.K. Choi and J. Harrigan, eds. Handbook of International Trade. Basil Blackwell, Oxford.

U.S. Census Bureau, 2008. Pollution Abatement Costs and Expenditures 2005.

Table 1: Aggregated GTAP Sectors and Regions

Sectors	Regions	
Grains and Crops	United States	Cyprus
Meats and Livestock	Oceania	Czech Republic
Extraction	China	France
Processed Food	Japan	Germany
Textiles and Wearing Apparel	Rest of East Asia	Greece
Electronics	Indonesia	Ireland
Machinery (other than Electronics)	Malaysia	Italy
Transportation Equipment	Philippines	Norway
Other Light Manufacturing	Singapore	Poland
Other Heavy Manufacturing	Rest of South East Asia	Portugal
Utilities and Construction	India	Russia
Transport Services	Rest of South Asia	Spain
Other Services	Canada	Switzerland
	Mexico	Turkey
Factor Endowments	Argentina	United Kingdom
Highly Skilled Labor	Brazil	Rest of Western Europe
Less Skilled Labor	Chile	Eastern Europe
Capital	Venezuela	Egypt
National Resources	Rest of South America	Rest of the Middle East
Land	Costa Rica	And Northern Africa
	Panama	Botswana
	Rest of Central America	Ethiopia
	and the Caribbean	South Africa
	Austria	Rest of Sub-Saharan Africa
	Belgium	Rest of the World

Table 2: Econometric Estimates of the Pareto Distribution Parameter γ

	Electronics Sector	Machinery Sector	Transportation Equipment Sector
Using the Freight and Import Duties Measure of Trade Costs			
Estimate of γ	9.897 (6.943 – 12.851)	6.419 (3.994 – 8.845)	7.271 (4.910 – 9.632)
R^2 Statistic	0.9884	0.9875	0.9687
F Statistic for the Region Fixed Effects	681.65	671.69	254.43
F Statistic for the Year Fixed Effects	6.81	25.54	10.33
Number of Observation	506	506	504
Using the Freight Only Measure of Trade Costs			
Estimate of γ	9.932 (6.957 – 12.907)	7.197 (4.808 – 9.586)	7.842 (5.482 – 10.202)
R^2 Statistic	0.9884	0.9877	0.9691
F Statistic for the Region Fixed Effects	672.75	654.62	241.42
F Statistic for the Year Fixed Effects	6.94	26.14	10.32
Number of Observation	506	506	504

Note: The 95% confidence intervals are reported in parentheses under the point estimates. All regressions include country fixed effects and year fixed effects.

Table 3: Pollution Abatement Costs in 2005

Reported in millions of dollars and as a share of the sector's annual total for each cost category.

	Electronics Sector	Machinery Sector	Transportation Equipment Sector
Labor Costs, including Contract Work	$329.8 million 0.4076%	$322.0 million 0.3518%	$699.4 million 0.5807%
Energy Costs	$142.4 million 5.5749%	$81.1 million 2.2732%	$377.1 million 8.3459%
Materials and Supplies	$86.2 million 0.0662%	$48.8 million 0.0252%	$102.5 million 0.0247%
Capital Expenditures	$155.9 million 0.9870%	$80.4 million 0.9226%	$260.1 million 1.7023%

Sources:

2005 Pollution Abatement Cost and Expenditures survey and 2005 Annual Survey of Manufactures,

U.S. Census Bureau.

Table 4: Economic Impact of the Sector's Pollution Abatement Labor Costs

	Electronics Sector	Machinery Sector	Transportation Equipment Sector
Labor Costs Associated with Pollution Abatement	$329.8 million	$322.0 million	$699.4 million
Value of U.S. Exports in the Sector (GTAP variable vxwfob)	-0.0545% -$67.6 million	-0.0030% -$3.7 million	-0.0135% -$19.9 million
Value of U.S. Imports in the Sector (GTAP variable viwcif)	0.0635% $174.6 million	0.0069% $11.8 million	0.1193% $305.3 million
U.S. Output in the Sector (GTAP variable qo)	-0.0787%	-0.0043%	-0.0955%
Sector Employment in the U.S. (GTAP variable qfe)			
Less Skilled Labor	0.0842%	0.0112%	0.2339%
Highly Skilled Labor	0.0840%	0.0110%	0.2339%
Number of Firms in the Sector That Sell in the U.S. Domestic Market	-0.9076%	-1.1803%	-0.9887%
Number of Firms in the Sector That Export from the United States			
to Canada	-0.0457%	-0.0700%	0.0565%
to the UK	-0.1899%	-0.0191%	-0.0969%
to Japan	-0.1826%	-0.0169%	-0.0663%
to Germany	-0.1933%	-0.0195%	-0.0831%
to China	-0.1489%	-0.0179%	-0.1018%
Profits of U.S. Producers in the Sector	-0.1574%	-0.0488%	-0.4474%

Table 5: Economic Impact of the Sector's Pollution Abatement Labor Costs Modeled as Variable, Rather Than Fixed, Costs of Production in the Transportation Sector

	Modeled as Fixed Costs in Extended Model	Modeled as Variable Costs in Extended Model	Modeled as Variable Costs in Standard Model
Value of U.S. Exports in the Sector (GTAP variable vxwfob)	-0.0135% -$19.9 million	-1.8859% -$2,830.3 million	-0.3724% -$550.4 million
Value of U.S. Imports in the Sector (GTAP variable viwcif)	0.1193% $305.3 million	0.2653% $677.8 million	0.1764% $451.1 million
U.S. Output in the Sector (GTAP variable qo)	-0.0955%	-0.8857%	-0.2770%
Sector Employment in the U.S. (GTAP variable qfe)			
Less Skilled Labor	0.2339%	-0.8171%	0.1564%
Highly Skilled Labor	0.2339%	-0.8171%	0.1557%

Table 6: Economic Impact of the Sector's Pollution Abatement Labor Costs Global Cost Shock Compared to Region-Specific Cost Shock in the Electronics Sector

	Region-Specific Cost Shock	Global Cost Shock
Value of U.S. Exports in the Sector (GTAP variable vxwfob)	-0.0545% -$67.6 million	0.0210% $26.1 million
Value of U.S. Imports in the Sector (GTAP variable viwcif)	0.0635% $174.6 million	0.0659% $181.1 million
U.S. Output in the Sector (GTAP variable qo)	-0.0787%	-0.0459%
Sector Employment in the United States (GTAP variable qfe)		
Less Skilled Labor	0.0842%	0.1361%
HighlySkilled Labor	0.0840%	0.1359%
Number of Firms in the Sector That Sell in the U.S. Domestic Market	-0.9076%	-0.8590%
Number of Firms in the Sector That Export from the United States		
to Canada	-0.0457%	0.0568%
to the UK	-0.1899%	-0.0165%
to Japan	-0.1826%	0.1926%
to Germany	-0.1933%	0.0050%
to China	-0.1489%	0.0171%
Profits of U.S. Producers in the Sector	-0.1574%	-0.1484%

Table 7: Economic Impact of the Sector's Pollution Abatement Labor Costs Global Cost Shock Compared to Region-Specific Cost Shock in the Machinery Sector

	Region-Specific Cost Shock	Global Cost Shock
Value of U.S. Exports in the Sector (GTAP variable vxwfob)	-0.0030% -$3.7 million	0.0009% $1.1 million
Value of U.S. Imports in the Sector (GTAP variable viwcif)	0.0069% $11.8 million	0.0070% $11.9 million
U.S. Output in the Sector (GTAP variable qo)	-0.0043%	-0.0034%
Sector Employment in the United States (GTAP variable qfe)		
Less Skilled Labor	0.0112%	0.0137%
Highly Skilled Labor	0.0110%	0.0135%
Number of Firms in the Sector That Sell in the U.S. Domestic Market	-1.1803%	-1.1791%
Number of Firms in the Sector That Export from the United States		
to Canada	-0.0700%	0.0039%
to the UK	-0.0191%	0.0044%
to Japan	-0.0169%	0.0168%
to Germany	-0.0195%	0.0061%
to China	-0.0179%	0.0150%
Profits of U.S. Producers in the Sector	-0.0488%	-0.0541%

Table 8: Economic Impact of the Sector's Pollution Abatement Labor Costs Global Cost Shock Compared to Region-Specific Cost Shock in the Transportation Equipment Sector

	Region-Specific Shock	Global Shock
Value of U.S. Exports in the Sector (GTAP variable vxwfob)	-0.0135% -$19.9 million	0.1943% $285.5 million
Value of U.S. Imports in the Sector (GTAP variable viwcif)	0.1193% $305.3 million	0.1251% $319.9 million
U.S. Output in the Sector (GTAP variable qo)	-0.0955%	-0.0215%
Sector Employment in the United States (GTAP variable qfe)		
Less Skilled Labor	0.2339%	0.3475%
Highly Skilled Labor	0.2339%	0.3481%
Number of Firms in the Sector That Sell in the U.S. Domestic Market	-0.9887%	-0.9207%
Number of Firms in the Sector That Export from the United States		
to Canada	0.0565%	0.3750%
to the UK	-0.0969%	0.3891%
to Japan	-0.0663%	0.5881%
to Germany	-0.0831%	0.3937%
to China	-0.1018%	0.7825%
Profits of U.S. Producers in the Sector	-0.4474%	-0.4628%

Table 9: Sensitivity of the Simulations to the Value of γ

	Electronics Sector	Machinery Sector	Transportation Equipment Sector
Baseline γ	**9.932**	**7.197**	**7.842**
Change in the Value of the Sector's U.S Exports	-0.0545% -$67.6 mil	-0.0030% -$3.7 mil	-0.0135% -$19.9 mil
Change in the Value of the Sector's U.S Imports	0.0635% $174.6 mil	0.0069% $11.8 mil	0.1193% $305.3 mil
γ at the Upper Bound of the 95% Confidence Interval	**12.907**	**9.586**	**10.202**
Change in the Value of the Sector's U.S Exports	-0.1560% -$193.8 mil	-0.0602% -$74.1 mil	-0.0306% -$45.1 mil
Change in the Value of the Sector's U.S Imports	0.0889% $244.1 mil	0.0846% $144.0 mil	0.1448% $370.4 mil

www.ingramcontent.com/pod-product-compliance
Lightning Source LLC
Chambersburg PA
CBHW081318180526
45170CB00007B/2764